how2become

KS3 Maths is Easy

(Working with Algebra)

www.How2Become.com

As part of this product you have also received FREE access to online tests that will help you to pass Key Stage 3 MATHS *(Working with Algebra)*.

To gain access, simply go to:

www.MyEducationalTests.co.uk

Get more products for passing any test at:

www.How2Become.com

Orders: Please contact How2Become Ltd, Suite 14, 50 Churchill Square Business Centre, Kings Hill, Kent ME19 4YU.

You can order through Amazon.co.uk under ISBN: 9781911259275, via the website www.How2Become.com or through Gardners.com.

ISBN: 9781911259275

First published in 2017 by How2Become Ltd.

Typeset by Katie Noakes for How2Become Ltd.

Disclaimer

Every effort has been made to ensure that the information contained within this guide is accurate at the time of publication. How2Become Ltd is not responsible for anyone failing any part of any selection process as a result of the information contained within this guide. How2Become Ltd and their authors cannot accept any responsibility for any errors or omissions within this guide, however caused. No responsibility for loss or damage occasioned by any person acting, or refraining from action, as a result of the material in this publication can be accepted by How2Become Ltd.

The information within this guide does not represent the views of any third party service or organisation.

Contains public sector information licensed under the Open Government Licence v3.0.

CONTENTS

UNDERSTANDING THE CURRICULUM

THE NATIONAL CURRICULUM

State-funded schools are governed by a set curriculum of 'core' subjects, which form part of a child's education. These core subjects are essential for providing key knowledge and skills, which in turn will help us to produce well-rounded and educated citizens.

In Key Stage 3 (ages 11-14), the core subjects that must be taught in schools include the following:

- **English**
- **Maths**
- **Science**
- **Art and Design**
- **Citizenship**
- **Computing**
- **Design and Technology**
- **Languages**
- **Geography**
- **History**
- **Music**
- **Physical Education**

All schools, from Key Stage 1 to Key Stage 4, must also teach Religious Studies to their students. From the age of 11, children will also be taught Sex Education. However, parents are given the option of pulling their children out from Religious Studies and Sex Education.

THE IMPORTANCE OF MATHS

Maths is an integral subject within the national curriculum. Students should be able to understand the key concepts and different mathematical formula, in order to enhance their knowledge and increase their cognitive ability.

By achieving a strong level of understanding, students are able to convey their mathematical knowledge in a range of other subjects, including science, computing, and geography.

The fundamental aims of the subject include:

- Using arithmetic to solve problems;
- Understanding the difference between accuracy and estimation;
- Expressing arithmetic using algebraic equations and formula;
- Learning how to carefully lay out sets of data using graphs and charts;
- Understanding averages in terms of mean, mode, median and range;
- Improving children's basic mathematical skills, before advancing on to more technical and challenging mathematical concepts;
- Improving children's confidence in their mathematical abilities, allowing them to grasp different topics of maths and how they can apply these techniques to their work.

In Key Stage 3, maths is broken down into several modules:

- **Numbers and Calculations;**
- **Ratio, Proportion and Rates of Change;**
- **Geometry and Measures;**
- **Working with Algebra;**
- **Probability and Statistics.**

The aforementioned modules are all used to teach students the vital skills for both academia and the outside world.

Pupils will be able to recognise different mathematical concepts and apply them to different calculations. In Key Stage 3, it is important that students are able to move fluently through the subject, and demonstrate a wide range of skills.

Key Stage 3 is a crucial time in academic terms, as it prepares students for their GCSEs. Every pupil will be required to take Maths as a GCSE, and therefore having a strong knowledge in these starter years at secondary school, will put students in the position that they are expected to be in before entering their GCSEs.

MATHS SUBJECT CONTENT

Below we have broken down the aims and objectives of each 'module' for Maths. This will hopefully give you some idea of what will be assessed, and how you can improve different areas in the mathematics subject.

PROBABILITY AND STATISTICS
<u>Pupils will be taught how to:</u> ☐ Understand the probability of an outcome. ☐ Record, describe and analyse the frequency of outcomes of simple probability experiments, involving randomness, fairness, equally and unequally outcomes, using mathematical language, and the use of a probability scale from 0-1. ☐ Enumerate data and understand information provided in the form of: ■ *Tables, grids, graphs and charts, Venn diagrams and pictograms.* ☐ Describe, interpret and compare information from graphical representations. ☐ Understand the mean, mode, median and range of a set of data, and comparing this to other similar data. ☐ Construct graphs and charts in order to represent a set of data. Pupils should understand what type of graph or chart works best for the data they have collated.

NUMBERS AND CALCULATIONS

Pupils will be taught how to:

☐ Apply the concepts of the following mathematical numbers:

- *Prime numbers, factors, multiples, common factors, common multiples, highest common factor (HCF), lowest common multiple (LCM) and prime factorisation.*

☐ Use place values for working out decimals, measures and integers of any size.

☐ Order numbers in terms of positive and negative. Students should also have a strong grasp of mathematical symbols including:

=, ≠, ≤, ≥

☐ Use brackets, powers, roots and reciprocals.

☐ Use different standard units of measure including:

- *Mass, length, time and money.*

☐ Round numbers up and down to the correct degree of accuracy. Students will be taught about significant figures and decimal places.

☐ Correctly use a calculator, and learn all of the key buttons on a scientific calculator.

☐ Interpret percentages as being 'a number out of 100'. Pupils will also be taught how to use percentages higher than 100%, how to convert a percentage into a fraction or decimal, and how to find the percentage of a number.

☐ Recognise square and cube numbers, and understand the importance of powers 2, 3, 4 and 5.

☐ Appreciate the infinite nature of the sets of integers, real and rational numbers.

☐ Interpret and compare numbers in standard form $A \times 10^N$ $1 \leq A < 10$, where N is a positive or negative integer or zero.

RATIO, PROPORTION AND RATES OF CHANGE

<u>Pupils will be taught how to:</u>

☐ Change between different standard units. For example:

- *Length, area, time volume and mass.*

☐ Use ratio notation, including reduction to simplest form.

☐ Use scale factors, scale diagrams and maps.

☐ Express one quantity as a fraction of another, where the fraction is less than 1 and greater than 1.

☐ Divide a given quantity into two parts in given part:part or part:whole ratio; express the division of a quantity into two parts as a ratio.

☐ Understand that a multiplicative relationship between two quantities can be expressed as a ratio or a fraction.

☐ Relate the language of ratios and the associated calculations to the arithmetic of fractions and to linear functions.

☐ Solve problems involving percentage change including:

- *Percentage increase, percentage decrease, original value problems and simple interest in financial mathematics.*

☐ Solve problems involving direct and inverse proportion, including graphical and algebraic representations.

☐ Using compound units such as speed, unit pricing and density to solve problems.

WORKING WITH ALGEBRA

Pupils will be taught how to:

☐ Use and interpret algebraic notations, including:

- *ab in place of a x b;*

- *3y in place of y + y + y and 3 x y;*

- *a^2 in place of a x a, a3 in place of a x a x a, a^2b in place of a x a x b;*

- *$^a/_b$ in place of a ÷ b;*

- *Coefficients written as fractions rather than as decimals;*

- *Brackets.*

☐ Substitute numerical values into formulae and expressions, including scientific formulae.

☐ Understand and use the concepts and vocabulary of expressions, equations, inequalities, terms and factors.

☐ Simplify and manipulate algebraic expressions to maintain equivalence by:

- *Collecting like terms;*

- *Multiplying a single term over a bracket;*

- *Taking out common factors;*

- *Expanding products of two or more binomials.*

☐ Recognise, sketch and produce graphs of linear and quadratic functions of one variable with appropriate scaling, using equations in x and y and the Cartesian plane.

☐ Use linear and quadratic graphs to estimate values of y for given values of x and vice versa and to find approximate solutions of simultaneous linear equations.

☐ Recognise arithmetic sequences and find the nth term.

☐ Find approximate solutions to contextual problems from given graphs of a variety of functions, including piece-wise linear, exponential and reciprocal graphs.

☐ Reduce a given linear equation in two variables to the standard form $y = mx + c$; calculate and interpret gradients and intercepts of graphs of such linear equations numerically, graphically and algebraically.

☐ Recognise geometric sequences and appreciate other sequences that arise.

GEOMETRY AND MEASURES

Pupils will be taught how to:

☐ Derive and apply formulae to calculate and solve problems involving;

- *Perimeter and area of triangles, parallelograms, trapezia, volume of cuboids (including cubes) and other prisms (including cylinders).*

☐ Calculate and solve problems involving: perimeters of 2D shapes (including circles), areas of circles and composite shapes.

☐ Draw and measure line segments and angles in geometric figures, including interpreting scale drawings.

☐ Derive and use the standard ruler and compass constructions (perpendicular bisector of a line segment, constructing a perpendicular to a given line from/at a given point, bisecting a given angle); recognise and use the perpendicular distance from a point to a line as the shortest distance to the line.

☐ Describe, sketch and draw using conventional terms and notations:

- *Points, lines, parallel lines, perpendicular lines, right angles, regular polygons, and other polygons that are reflectively and rotationally symmetric.*

☐ Use the standard convention for labelling the sides and angles of triangle ABC, and know and use the criteria for congruence of triangles.

☐ Derive and illustrate properties of triangles, quadrilaterals, circles and other place figures [for example, equal lengths and angles] using appropriate language and technologies.

☐ Use Pythagoras' Theorem and trigonometric ratios in similar triangles to solve problems involving right-angled triangles.

☐ Use properties of faces, surfaces, edges and vertices of cubes, cuboids, prisms, cylinders, pyramids, cones and spheres to solve problems in 3D.

☐ Interpret mathematical relationships both algebraically and geometrically.

☐ Identify properties of, and describe the results of, translations, rotations and reflections applied to given figures.

☐ Identify and construct triangles, and construct congruent triangles, and construct similar shapes by enlargements, with and without coordinate grids.

☐ Apply the properties of angles at a point, angles at a point on a straight line, vertically opposite angles.

☐ Understand and use the relationship between parallel lines and alternate and corresponding angles.

Maths is not only a core subject in schools, but is also a topic that impacts upon every aspect of our daily lives. As you can see, it is imperative that students are able to engage in mathematics, in order to improve on vital skills and knowledge.

USING THIS GUIDE

This guide focuses specifically on Key Stage 3 Maths *(Working with Algebra)*. This book will cover everything you need to know in terms of algebra and equations.

REMEMBER – It's important that you have a good mathematical understanding, as this will help you through other school subjects, and in day-to-day activities.

HOW WILL I BE ASSESSED?

At Key Stage 3, children will be assessed based on Levels. These years do not count towards anything, and are simply a reflection of progression and development. The first years of secondary school are in place in order to determine whether or not pupils are meeting the minimum requirements, and are therefore an integral stage for preparing pupils for their GCSE courses.

Although these years do not count towards any final results, they do go a long way in deciphering which GCSEs you will pick up. For example, if you were excelling in Maths at KS3, you could consider taking this subject at A Level, and even Higher Education!

The subjects that you choose at GCSE will impact upon your future aspirations, including further education and career opportunities.

You will be monitored and assessed throughout these schooling years, via the following:

• Ongoing teacher assessments;

• Term progress reports;

• Summative assessments at the end of each academic year.

By the end of Key Stage 3, pupils are expected to achieve Levels 5 or 6.

INCREASE YOUR CHANCES

Below is a list of GOLDEN NUGGETS that will help YOU and your CHILD to prepare for Key Stage 3 Maths.

Golden Nugget 1 – Revision timetables

When it comes to revising, preparation is key. That is why you need to sit down with your child and come up with an efficient and well-structured revision timetable.

It is important that you work with your child to assess their academic strengths and weaknesses, in order to carry out these revision sessions successfully.

TIP – Focus on their weaker areas first!

TIP – Create a weekly revision timetable to work through different subject areas.

TIP – Spend time revising with your child. Your child will benefit from your help and this is a great way for you to monitor their progress.

Golden Nugget 2 – Understanding the best way your child learns

There are many different ways to revise when it comes to exams, and it all comes down to picking a way that your child will find most useful.

Below is a list of the common learning styles that you may want to try with your child:

- **Visual** – the use of pictures and images to remember information.

- **Aural** – the use of sound and music to remember information.

- **Verbal** – the use of words, in both speech and writing, to understand information.

- **Social** – working together in groups.

- **Solitary** – working and studying alone.

Popular revision techniques include: *mind mapping, flash cards, making notes, drawing flow charts,* and *diagrams*. You could instruct your child on how to turn diagrams and pictures into words, and words into diagrams. Try as many different methods as possible, to see which style your child learns from the most.

TIP – Work out what kind of learner your child is. What method will they benefit from the most?

TIP – Try a couple of different learning aids and see if you notice a change in your child's ability to understand what is being taught.

Golden Nugget 3 – Break times

Allow your child plenty of breaks when revising.

It's really important not to overwork your child.

TIP – Practising for 10 to 15 minutes per day will improve your child's reading ability.

TIP – Keep in mind that a child's retention rate is usually between 30 to 50 minutes. Any longer than this, and your child will start to lose interest.

Golden Nugget 4 – Practice, practice and more practice!

Purchase past practice papers. This is a fantastic way for you to gain an idea of how your child is likely to be tested.

Golden Nugget 5 – Understanding different areas in Maths

As with any subject, Maths has a range of different modules. Therefore, your child may find one module easier than another. We recommend that you spend time focusing on one module at a time. This will ensure that your child knows everything they should about each module – before moving on to the next.

TIP – Know what modules you need to focus on!

Golden Nugget 6 – Improve their confidence

Encourage your child to interact with you, their peers and their teachers. If they are struggling, they need to be able to reach out and ask for help. By asking for help, they will be able to work on their weaknesses, and therefore increase their overall performance and confidence.

> *TIP – Talk to your child and work through different Maths questions with them.*

Golden Nugget 7 – Stay positive!

The most important piece of preparation advice we can give you, is to make sure that your child is positive and relaxed about these tests.

Don't let assessments worry you, and certainly don't let them worry your child.

> *TIP – Make sure the home environment is as comfortable and relaxed as possible for your child.*

Golden Nugget 8 – Answer the easier questions first

A good tip to teach your child is to answer all the questions they find easiest first. That way, they can swiftly work through the paper, before attempting the questions they struggle with.

> *TIP – Get your child to undergo a practice paper. Tell them to fill in the answers that they find the easiest first. That way, you can spend time helping your child with the questions they find more difficult.*
>
> *Spend some time working through the questions they find difficult and make sure that they know how to work out the answer.*

Golden Nugget 9 – Understanding mathematical terminology

The next section is a glossary containing all the mathematical terminology that your child should familiarise themselves with.

Sit down with your child and learn as many of these KEY TERMS as you can.

> *TIP – Why not make your child's learning fun? Write down all of the terms and cut them out individually. Do the same for the definitions.*
>
> *Get your child to try and match the KEY TERM with its definition. Keep playing this game until they get them all right!*

Golden Nugget 10 – Check out our other revision resources

We have a range of other KS3 Maths resources to help your child prepare for EVERY stage of their mathematical learning.

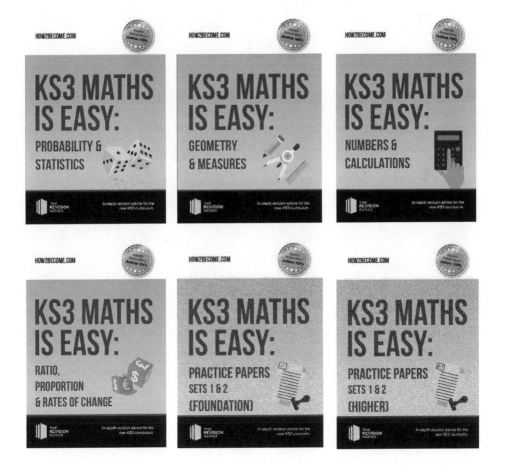

LEARN YOUR
MATHS
TERMINOLOGY

ACUTE ANGLES	An angle less than 90°.
ALGEBRA	The part of maths where symbols and letters are used to represent numbers.
AREA	A measurement of a surface. For the area of a square, you would multiply the height by the width.
BIDMAS	**B**rackets, **I**ndices, **D**ivision, **M**ultiplication, **A**ddition, **S**ubtraction – order of operations.
CIRCUMFERENCE	The distance around something. It is the enclosing boundary of a curved geometric figure.
COMPOUND SHAPE	A compound shape includes two or more simple shapes.
CUBED NUMBERS	A cubed number is a number multiplied by itself, three times.
DECIMAL PLACES	The position of a digit to the right of a decimal point.
DECIMAL	A type of number, for example 0.5 is equivalent to 50%.
DIAMETER	A straight line passing side-to-side through the middle of a circle.
EQUILATERAL TRIANGLE	A type of triangle. All sides and angles are of equal value. All angles are 60°.
ESTIMATION	A rough calculation or guess.
FACTOR	A factor is a number that can be divided wholly into another number. For example, 4 is a factor of 8.
FRACTIONS	A type of number, for example ½ is equivalent to a half.
FREQUENCY	The frequency of a specific data is the number of times that number occurs (Frequent).
HIGHEST COMMON FACTOR (HCF)	To find the HCF, you need to find all of the factors of two or more numbers, and then see which number is the highest.

IMPERIAL UNITS	Imperial units of length, mass and capacity. Includes inch, foot, yard, ounce, pound, stone, pint and gallon.
ISOSCELES TRIANGLE	A type of triangle. Two sides and angles are of the same value.
LOWEST COMMON MULTIPLE (LCM)	To find the LCM, you need to find all of the multiples of two or more numbers, and then work out the lowest number in common.
MEAN	A type of average. Add up all of the numbers and divide it by how many numbers there are.
MEDIAN	A type of average. Rearrange the numbers in ascending order. What number is in the middle?
METRIC UNITS	Metric units of length, mass and capacity. Includes mm, cm, km, mg, g, kg, ml and litres.
MODE	A type of average. What number occurs the most?
MULTIPLE	A multiple simply means 'times tables'. The multiples of 2 are 2, 4, 6, 8 and so on.
NEGATIVE NUMBER	A negative number is a number less than 0. On a scale, positive numbers move to the right, and negative numbers move to the left. Indicated by the sign '-'. For example, -4.
OBTUSE ANGLE	A type of angle. An obtuse angle is more than 90° but less than 180°.
PARALLEL LINE	A parallel line is two or more lines that are always the same distance apart, and never touch.
PERIMETER	A measurement of a surface. The line forming the boundary of a closed geometrical figure.
PERPENDICULAR LINES	A perpendicular line is two lines that meet at a right angle (90°).
PI	The mathematic constant 3.14159... The ratio of a circle's circumference to its diameter.

POSITIVE NUMBER	A positive number is a number more than 0. On a scale, positive numbers move to the right, and negative numbers move to the left.
PROBABILITY	The extent to whether something is likely to occur.
RADIUS	The radius is a straight line.
RANGE	A type of average. The range between the largest number and the smallest number.
RATIO	The quantitative relation between two amounts showing the number of times one value contain or is contained within the other.
REFLEX ANGLE	A type of angle. A reflex angle is more than 180° but less than 360°.
RIGHT-ANGLED TRIANGLE	A type of triangle. A triangle that has a 90° angle.
SCALENE TRIANGLE	A triangle with no equal angles or equal length sides.
SIGNIFICANT FIGURES	The digits carrying meaning. This allows us get a rough idea. For example, 48,739. The '4' is a significant figure because it represents 40 thousand.
SIMPLIFYING FRACTIONS	A way of making a fraction easier to read by finding a whole number that can be divided equally into both the denominator and numerator. For example, 12/24 can be simplified to 1/2. Both '12' and '24' can be divided by 12.
SQUARED NUMBER	A square number is the number that is reached when multiplying two of the same numbers together. For example 9 is the square number of 3 x 3.
SYMMETRY	Symmetry is when one shape becomes exactly like another if it's flipped or rotated.
VOLUME	The amount of space that a shape or object occupies. Contained within a container.

UNDERSTANDING

ALGEBRA

(INTRODUCTION TO ALGEBRA)

UNDERSTANDING ALGEBRA

Algebra is a part of mathematics which substitutes numbers with letters and symbols.

You need to be able to work out what the letters and symbols are representing. Without knowing what they represent, you will struggle to work out the correct answers.

Algebra can be broken up into different topics, all of which will be covered in this guide. Topics include the following:

- Collecting like terms;

- Multiplying out brackets;

- Adding and subtracting algebra;

- Simplifying equations;

- Inequalities;

- Simultaneous equations;

- Number, linear, and quadratic sequences;

- Coordinates and graphs.

Below we have provided some very basic algebra, just to give you a bit more of an insight into what is meant in regards to algebra and formulas.

1	2	3	4	5	6	7	8	9	10
A	B	C	D	E	F	G	H	I	J

EXAMPLES

Question 1

Work out the formula:

$D + F + B$

- $D = 4$
- $F = 6$
- $B = 2$
- So, 4 + 6 + 2 = 12

Question 2

Work out the formula:

$5E + 3G$

- $E = 5 = (5 \times 5) = 25$
- $G = 7 = (7 \times 3) = 21$
- 25 + 21 = 46

TOP TIP!
If you have a number BEFORE a letter, that means that you have to multiply that number by the letter.

Instead of using letters to replace numbers, you can also use symbols!

This works in exactly the same way. Remember, you will often be asked questions that require you to work out what the symbol is representing.

EXAMPLE

Work out the formula:

$$7 + \bigstar = 15$$

- The star is representing a number. Your job is to work out what that number is.

- If 7 add the star equals 15, that means the star is = 15 - 7 = 8.

- If we factor the number 8 back in the sequence, we get = 7 + 8 = 15.

TOP TIP!

If you are trying to work out the missing symbol, the best tip is to work backwards.

In the above example, use the answer to subtract the number you already know, to work out the number that is missing.

NOTE = you will always do the OPPOSITE operation to what it says in the question.

Question Time!

QUESTION 1

If $a = 8$, $b = 6$ and $c = 4$, work out the following equations:

a) $2b + c$

b) $6 + bc$

c) $2b - c$

d) $2a + 3b + c$

e) $7c - a$

f) $9c \div b$

QUESTION 2

Work out the following symbols:

a) 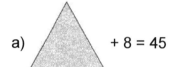 + 8 = 45

b) ⌐ x 4 = 28

c) 36 ÷ ⬤ = 12

d) 121 = ⬇ + 56

QUESTION 3

Work out the following letters:

a) $35 - t = 17$

b) $r \div 5 = 8$

c) $n^2 = 49$

d) $k + 6 - 3 = 15$

e) $6h = 90$

f) $(4 \times m) + (m^2) = 60$

QUESTION 4

Using the following table, work out the answers to the questions below.

1	2	3	4	5	6	7	8	9	10
A	B	C	D	E	F	G	H	I	J

a) $3J + 4D$

b) $12E \times 2B$

c) $D \times F \times H$

QUESTION 5

Complete the wordsearch below.

Sequences	*Symbols*	*Numbers*
Inqualities	*Algebra*	*Formula*
Letters	*Patterns*	*Simplifying*
Terms	*Linear*	*Quadratic*
Simultaneous	*Equations*	

```
D  N  C  L  S  I  S  G  S  H  Z  N  Q  A  Q

O  K  I  P  I  N  Y  E  Y  Y  Y  M  L  H  X

J  O  T  J  W  E  S  X  C  Y  M  G  L  S  J

U  P  A  V  E  Q  I  R  B  N  E  B  I  K  S

B  J  R  N  S  U  H  N  E  B  E  M  O  N  M

R  C  D  G  G  A  Q  Q  R  T  U  U  O  L  R

N  R  A  B  G  L  V  A  X  L  T  I  Q  D  S

U  A  U  D  C  I  M  G  T  L  T  E  J  E  J

M  E  Q  D  S  T  P  A  Q  A  M  I  L  Y  S

B  N  O  F  S  I  N  X  U  C  L  Q  P  Q  F

E  I  L  M  E  E  Z  Q  A  L  U  M  R  O  F

R  L  R  C  O  S  E  P  A  T  T  E  R  N  S

S  E  A  U  G  N  I  Y  F  I  L  P  M  I  S

T  T  S  R  F  Q  N  V  Q  D  Y  Y  J  X  Z

Z  D  Z  R  O  U  I  B  K  M  Q  D  H  P  E
```

Answers

Q1.

a) **16**

- $(2 \times 6 = 12)$
- $12 + 4 = 16$

b) **30**

- $6 + (6 \times 4)$
- $6 + 24 = 30$

c) **8**

- $(2 \times 6 = 12)$
- $12 - 4 = 8$

d) **38**

- $(2 \times 8 = 16)$
- $(3 \times 6 = 18)$
- $16 + 18 + 4 = 38$

e) **20**

- $(7 \times 4 = 28)$
- $28 - 8 = 20$

f)   6

- (9 x 4 = 36)
- 36 ÷ 6 = 6

Q2.

a)   △ = 37

- 45 - 8 = 37

b)   ⌐ = 7

- 28 ÷ 4 = 7

c)   ◎ = 3

- 36 ÷ 12 = 3

d)   ⬇ = 65

- 121 - 56 = 65

Q3.

a) $t = 18$

- 35 - 18 = 17

b) $r = 40$

- 5 x 8 = 40

c)   *n* = 7

- Square root of 49 = 7

d)   *k* = 12

- (6 - 3 = 3)
- 15 - 3 = 12

e)   *h* = 15

- 90 ÷ 6 = 15

f)   *m* = 6

- (4 x 6 = 24)
- (6 x 6 = 36)
- 24 + 36 = 60

Q4.

a)   **46**

- (3 x 10 = 30)
- (4 x 4 = 16)
- 30 + 16 = 46

b)   **240**

- (12 x 5 = 60)
- (2 x 2 = 4)
- 60 x 4 = 240

c)   192

- 4 x 6 x 8 = 192

Q5.

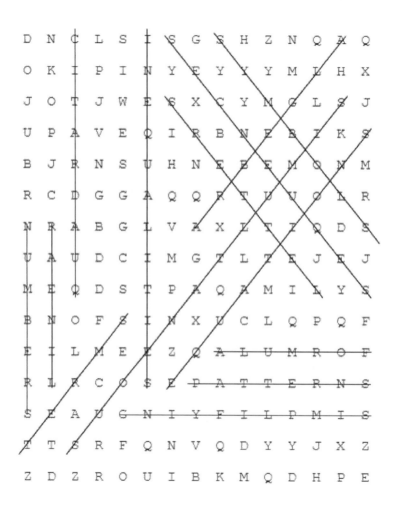

COLLECTING LIKE TERMS

TERMS

(INTRODUCTION TO ALGEBRA)

COLLECTING LIKE TERMS

The word 'term' is used to describe the different parts of an expression.

These can include NUMBERS, LETTERS and BRACKETS.

Every term is separated by operation signs such as +, -, x or ÷. If there is no sign in front of the term, that means there is an INVISIBLE + sign.

EXAMPLE 1

As you can see, the first term does not have an operation shown. However, this means that there is an INVISIBLE + sign.

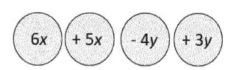

Using the expression in the above example, you can see that there are two different expressions - the terms that have the letter '*x*', and the terms that have the letter '*y*'.

That means we can simplify the expression as follows:

- The '*x*' terms can be collected together to give 11*x*.

- The '*y*' terms can be collected together to give -1*y*.

NOTE

The word SIMPLIFYING means the SAME as 'COLLECTING LIKE TERMS'.

There is a simple way to simplify an expression, or collecting like terms, and that is by grouping.

EXAMPLE 2

Simplify the expression:

$$7x + 3 + 3y - 2x + 8 + 6y$$

- $(7x)$ $(+3)$ $(+3y)$ $(-2x)$ $(+8)$ $(+6y)$
- $(7x - 2x) = 5x$
- $(+3 + 8) = +11$
- $(+3y + 6y) = +9y$

So, the answer is:

$5x + 11 + 9y$

NOTE

When it comes to grouping, you must remember to group the operations with the correct term.

The operation will always be in front of the term.

ACTIVITY TIME!

Simplify:

a) $6y + x - 4y - 3$

b) $7x + 5y + 4 + x + 4z - 3y$

SIMPLIFYING TERMS - MORE ADVANCED!

So far, we've learnt the basics of simplifying terms, and this has been relatively easy!

However, there are some rules you need to be aware of in order to simplify more complicated expressions.

WORKING WITH NEGATIVE NUMBERS

Sometimes, expressions will require you to work with negative numbers. This is nothing to be afraid of, and is quite simple if you know what to do with the symbols.

+ and a +	*+ multiply -*	*+ multiply +*
+	**-**	**+**
- and a -	*- multiply +*	*- multiply -*
+	**-**	**+**
+ and a -	*+ divided by -*	*+ divided by +*
-	**-**	**+**
- and a +	*- divided by +*	*- divided by -*
-	**-**	**+**

- *When the signs are different, the answer will be negative.*

- *When the signs are the same, the answer will be positive.*

RULES YOU NEED TO REMEMBER!

There are lots of combinations used in algebraic expressions, so you need to know the rules when using letters, symbols and operation signs.

RULE 1

When you have letters placed together, (*abc*) or a number with a letter (*3x*), that means you need to MULTIPLY.

- *abc* means *a* x *b* x *c*

- *3b* means 3 x *b*

RULE 2

When using powers, these tell you how many times something is multiplied.

- $7^8 = 7 \times 7 \times 7 \times 7 \times 7 \times 7 \times 7 \times 7$

- $t^5 = t \times t \times t \times t \times t$

RULE 3

When multiplying something by a power, you need to make sure you are multiplying the correct letters.

- $ab^2 = a \times b \times b$

  (You do NOT multiply the *a* by the power)

- $(ab)^2 = a \times a \times b \times b$

  (You would multiply everything in the brackets by the power)

RULE 4

Powers are quite straightforward, but you need to make sure you know what to do with them when multiplying or dividing.

- When multiplying, you will add the powers.

- When dividing, you will subtract the powers.

- When a power is being raised by another power, you will multiply.

Question Time!

QUESTION 1

Simplify the following expression:

$$2k + 3k + 4g - 3g$$

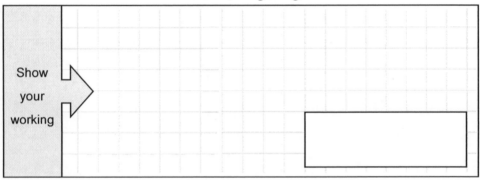

Show your working

QUESTION 2

Simplify the following expression:

$$t^2 + 5c + 4s - c + 2s$$

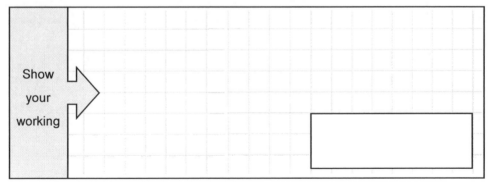

Show your working

QUESTION 3

Simplify the following expression:

$$5y + 6y - 3 - 4y + 8$$

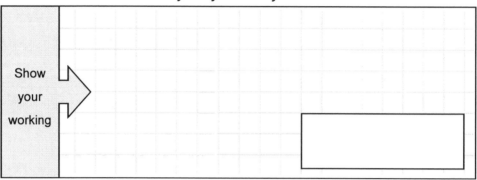

QUESTION 4

Simplify the following expression:

$$3x^2 + 11x + 4 - 3x + 7$$

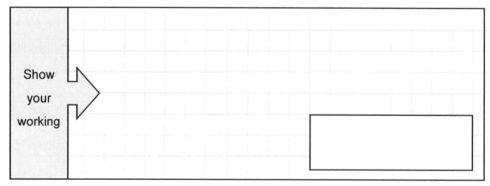

QUESTION 5

For the following statements, circle whether they are **true** or **false**.

a) In regards to algebraic expressions, **y** means **1y.**

TRUE / **FALSE**

b) The first term in an expression has no operation in front of it. The invisible operation is always a minus sign.

TRUE / **FALSE**

c) $a \times a \times a$ is the same as $3a$.

TRUE / **FALSE**

QUESTION 6

Simplify the following:

1. $a^7 \times a^9$

_____

2. $m^{11} \div m^7$

_____

3. $\dfrac{h^{18}}{h^5}$

_____

4. $a \times a \times a \times a \times a$

_____

5. $a \times b \times b \times b$

_____

Answers

Q1.

5k + g

- (2*k*) (+3*k*) (+4*g*) (-3*g*)

- 2*k* + 3*k* = 5*k*

- +4*g* - 3*g* = 1*g*

- 5*k* + *g*

Q2.

t^2 + 4c + 6s

- (t^2) (+5*c*) (+4*s*) (-*c*) (+2*s*)

- +5*c* - *c* = +4*c*

- +4*s* + 2*s* = +6*s*

- t^2 + 4*c* + 6*s*

Q3.

7y + 5

- (5*y*) (+6*y*) (-3) (-4*y*) (+8)

- 5*y* + 6*y* - 4*y* = 7*y*

- -3 + 8 = +5

- 7*y* + 5

Q4.

$3x^2 + 8x + 11$

- $(3x^2)$ $(+11x)$ $(+4)$ $(-3x)$ $(+7)$

- $+11x - 3x = +8x$

- $+4 + 7 = +11$

- $3x^2 + 8x + 11$

Q5.

a) true

b) false

c) false

Q6.

1. a^{16}

2. m^4

3. h^{13}

4. a^5

5. ab^3

HOW ARE YOU GETTING ON?

MULTIPLYING OUT BRACKETS

(INTRODUCTION TO ALGEBRA)

MULTIPLYING OUT BRACKETS

Something that you will HAVE to learn is how to multiply out brackets.

Multiplying brackets is quite a tricky thing to get your head around.

There are a few things that you can learn to make your life easier when it comes to multiplying out brackets:

1. The most important thing to remember is that everything INSIDE the bracket should be multiplied by the term (or number) OUTSIDE of the bracket.

2. If there is a minus sign OUTSIDE of the bracket, that will REVERSE all of the signs when multiplying.

EXAMPLE 1

$2(y + 5)$
- $(2 \times y) + (2 \times 5)$
- $2y + 10$

EXAMPLE 2

$6(2y + 6)$
- $(6 \times 2y) + (6 \times 6)$
- $12y + 36$

As you can see from the examples on the previous page, you are multiplying the term outside of the bracket with EVERYTHING that is inside the brackets.

This process is called **EXPANDING.** If a question asks you to expand the brackets, that means you need to follow the same process just shown.

Sometimes, you will be given more than one bracket. For these types of questions, you will have to **EXPAND** and **SIMPLIFY.**

EXAMPLE 1

$3(a + b) + 2(a + b)$
- $(3a + 3b) + (2a + 2b)$
- $5a + 5b$

EXAMPLE 2

$(y - 1) (3y + 4)$

- $(y \times 3y) + (y \times 4) + (-1 \times 3y) + (-1 \times 4)$
    $3y^2$ $+ 4y$ $-3y$ -4
- $3y^2 + 1y - 4$

Question Time!

QUESTION 1

Expand and simplify:

$$10(y + 2) + 2(y + 6)$$

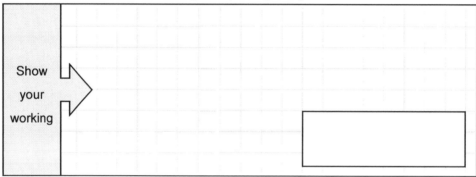

Show your working

QUESTION 2

Multiply out:

$$(x - 10)^2$$

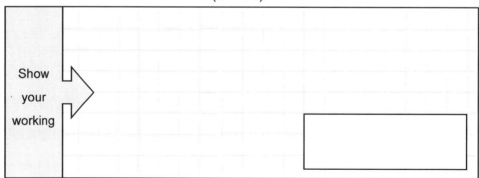

Show your working

QUESTION 3

Multiply out:

$$-5(5a^2 - 8b^2)$$

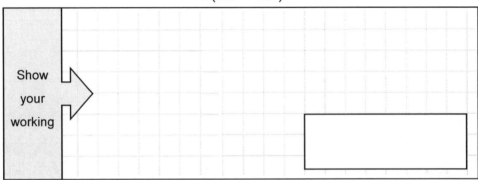

QUESTION 4

Expand and simplify:

$$8(2a + 8) + 4(9a - 3)$$

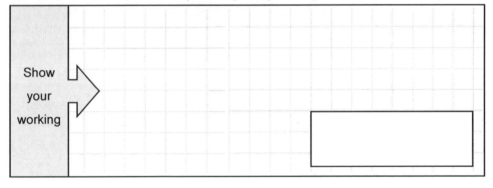

QUESTION 5

Expand and simplify:

$$9(x + 5) - 3(x - 8)$$

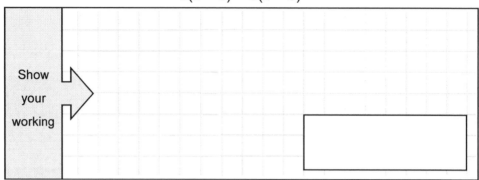

Show your working

QUESTION 6

Expand the following:

1. $-y(3y + 4)$

_____

_____

2. $5y(x - 4a)$

_____

_____

3. $-4(6a^2 - 5x^2)$

_____

_____

Answers

Q1.

12y + 32

- 10(y + 2) + 2(y + 6)
- 10y + 20 + 2y + 12
- 10y + 2y = 12y
- +12 + 20 = + 32
- 12y + 32

Q2.

x^2 - 20x + 100

- (x - 10) (x - 10)
- x^2 - 10x - 10x + 100
- x^2 - 20x + 100

Q3.

-25a^2 + 40b^2

- -5 x 5a^2 = -25a^2
- -5 x -8b^2 = 40b^2
- -25a^2 + 40b^2

Q4.

52a + 52

- 16*a* + 64 + 36*a* - 12
- 16*a* + 36*a* = 52*a*
- 64 - 12 = 52
- 52*a* + 52

Q5.

6x + 69

- 9*x* + 45 - 3*x* + 24
- 9*x* - 3*x* = 6*x*
- 45 + 24 = 69
- 6*x* + 69

Q6.

1. **$-3y^2 - 4y$**
2. **5yx - 20ya**
3. **$-24a^2 + 20x^2$**

FACTORISING

(INTRODUCTION TO ALGEBRA)

FACTORISING

> **Factorising is the process of putting brackets back in to expressions.**

In the previous chapter, we looked at how to expand brackets to remove them from the expression.

Now, we are looking at the exact opposite. We are looking at how to put brackets back in!

EXAMPLE 1

Factorise:

$$4y - 8$$

How to factorise:

- First of all, you need to find the highest common factor. This will either be a number or term.

- The common factor will be placed on the outside of the bracket. The numbers and terms inside the brackets will be multiplied by the outside term.

4y - 8

- 4 and 8 are both divisible by 4. So, the number 4 will be placed outside of the brackets.

- Next, you need to work out what you need to multiply by the 4 in order to get the rest of the expression.

$$4(y - 2)$$

If you expand this answer, you should reach the expression we first started with: $4y - 8$.

As we mentioned, sometimes the number on the outside of the bracket might not always be a number - it might be a letter instead.

EXAMPLE 2

Factorise:

$$x^2 - 4x$$

How to factorise:

- Use the same process that we just learned. You will need to find the highest common factor.

- The common factor will be placed on the outside of the bracket. The numbers and terms inside the brackets will be multiplied by the outside term.

$x^2 - 4x$

- Both parts of the expression can be divided by x. So, this term will be placed outside of the brackets.

- Next, you need to work out what you need to multiply by the x in order to get the rest of the expression.

$$x(x - 4)$$

If you expand this answer, you should reach the expression we first started with: $x^2 - 4x$.

REMEMBER!

- Find the highest common factor. This will be positioned outside of the brackets.

- Using the common factor, you will be able to work out what needs to be multiplied in order to get the original expression.

- Always make sure that you check your answer by multiplying out the brackets (just like you learned in the previous chapter!)

Question Time!

QUESTION 1

Factorise:

$$18x^2 - 12$$

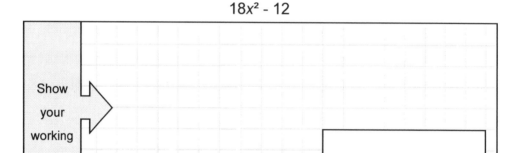

QUESTION 2

Factorise:

$$x^2 - 64$$

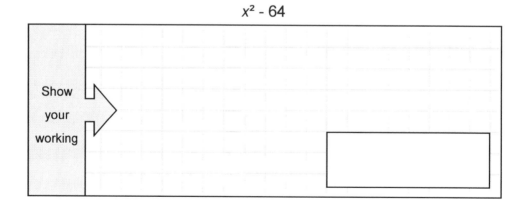

QUESTION 3

Factorise:

$$64a^2 - 81b^2$$

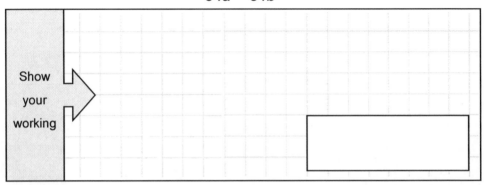

QUESTION 4

Factorise:

$$4ab - 8a^2$$

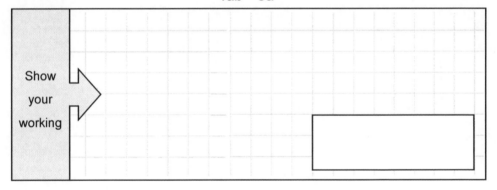

QUESTION 5

Factorise:

$$49a^2 - 25b^2$$

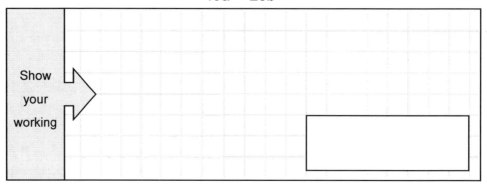

QUESTION 6

Factorise:

$$20a^2 - 10a$$

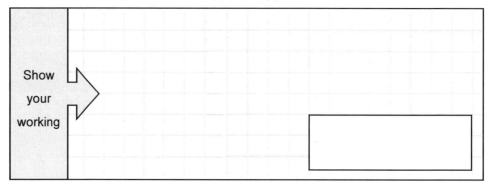

Answers

Q1.

$6(3x^2 - 2)$

- The highest common factor between 18 and 12 is 6. This will be placed outside of the brackets.

- $6 \times 3x^2 = 18x^2$

- $6 \times -2 = -12$

Q2.

$(x - 8) (x + 8)$

- $(x)^2 - (8)^2$

- $(x - 8) (x + 8)$

Q3.

$(8a - 9b) (8a + 9b)$

- Both 64 and 81 are square numbers.

- $(8a)^2 + (9b)^2$

- $(8a - 9b) (8a + 9b)$

Q4.

$4a(b - 2a)$

- The common factor between 4 and 8 is 4. Both parts of the expression also has the term a in common too.

- So 4a will be positioned outisde of the bracket.

- Using $4a$, you will be able to work out what numbers and terms will be placed inside of the brackets.

Q5.

$(7a - 5b) (7a + 5b)$

- Both 49 and 25 are square numbers.

- $(7a)^2 - (5b)^2$

- $(7a - 5b) (7a + 5b)$

Q6.

$10a (2a - 1)$

- The common factor of 20 and 10 is 10. So this number will go outside of the brackets.

HOW ARE YOU GETTING ON?

UNDERSTANDING EQUATIONS

(INTRODUCTION TO EQUATIONS)

UNDERSTANDING EQUATIONS

Equations and expressions are very different.

Equations are made up of two expressions, one either side of an equals sign.

When dealing with equations, you will need to work out the value of a missing number.

EXAMPLE

$x + 4 = 9$

- For the equation above, 'x' is the value we are missing. You need to work out its value.

- In this case, we can work out the value of 'x' by working backwards:

  $9 - 4 = 5$

- We would minus the 4, because the operation would need to be reversed.

- If we factor in this value into the equation, we would get:

  $5 + 4 = 9$

An algebraic equation is an equation that involves letters.

These letters represent a number, and it's up to you to work out the missing values in the equations.

Now you know what equations are, you will be expected to handle equations with confidence.

The following chapters will teach you more complex equations:

- Balancing equations (page 77)

- Solving equations (page 85)

- Simultaneous equations (page 93)

This chapter is simply the basics... just to get you started!

Have a go at the activity questions on the next few pages, before moving on to slightly trickier equations and concepts.

ACTIVITY TIME!

For the following equations, work out the value of x.

a) $9 - x = 5$

b) $120 \div x = 20$

c) $x = 30 \times 20$

d) $2x \times 6 = 48$

Question Time!

QUESTION 1

On the right are six equations. On the left is the value of x. Match the equation with the correct value.

$x + 9 = 24$	312
$x \div 2 = 156$	9
$2x = 72$	12
$8x = 72$	15
$6x + 7 = 79$	-11
$x + 3 = -8$	36

QUESTION 2

Give one example of an expression, and one example of an equation.

Expression =

Equation =

QUESTION 3

Below are 12 rectangular boxes. Each of these contains an equation.

There are four possible answer choices. Each answer choice is assigned with a colour.

For each equation, colour in the rectangle box, based on the colour choice of the answer.

$x = 4$	$x = 5$	$x = 8$	$x = 2$
(BLUE)	*(PINK)*	*(GREEN)*	*(RED)*

$9 + x = 14$	$4x + 4 = 20$	$72 \div x = 36$	$-3 + x = 2$
$x - 6 = 2$	$3x = 12$	$-2 + x = 0$	$x - 6 = -4$
$5x + 3 = 43$	$x + x + 7 = 11$	$20x + 5x = 100$	$11x = 88$

QUESTION 4

Solve the equations:

1. $x + 11 = 33$ $x = $ _____

2. $5x + 3x = 16$ $x = $ _____

3. $x \div 9 = 6$ $x = $ _____

4. $x + x + x + x = 52$ $x = $ _____

Answers

Q1.

- $x + 9 = 24$ $x = 15$
- $x \div 2 = 156$ $x = 312$
- $2x = 72$ $x = 36$
- $8x = 72$ $x = 9$
- $6x + 7 = 79$ $x = 12$
- $x + 3 = -8$ $x = -11$

Q2.

You could have any answer, as long as you have demonstrated an expression and an equation correctly. Remember, an expression DOES NOT contain an equals sign, whereas an equation DOES have an equals sign.

For example:

Expression = $5a + 5b + 3 + a$

Equation = $5b = 20$

Q3.

BLUE *(x = 4)*	PINK *(x = 5)*	GREEN *(x = 8)*	RED *(x = 2)*
$4x + 4 = 20$	$9 + x = 14$	$x - 6 = 2$	$72 \div x = 36$
$3x = 12$	$-3 + x = 2$	$5x + 3 = 43$	$-2 + x = 0$
$20x + 5x = 100$		$11x = 88$	$x - 6 = -4$
			$x + x + 7 = 11$

Q4.

1. x = 22

- 33 - 11 = 22

2. x = 2

- (5 x 2) + (3 x 2) = 16

3. x = 54

- 9 x 6 = 54

4. x = 13

- 52 ÷ 4 = 13

HOW ARE YOU GETTING ON?

BALANCING EQUATIONS

(INTRODUCTION TO EQUATIONS)

BALANCING EQUATIONS

When we think of an equation, we need to think of a balance beam or balancing scale!

Both sides of an equation must BALANCE. Each expression on either side of the equals sign is representing the same value.

To solve an equation, you will need to work out all of the missing values. There may be more than one missing value.

GOLDEN NUGGETS

1. Whatever you do to one side of the equation, you must do to the other side.

2. Often, you will need to get rid of something on one side, to work out the missing value. To get rid of something, you must do the opposite to what it is saying (if the equation uses a +, you will -. If the equation uses a ÷, you will x.)

3. You will need to keep getting rid of values, until you are left with one letter.

Question Time!

QUESTION 1

The balance bar is balancing exactly. Using the equation, work out the value of *a*.

$$a + 11 \qquad = \qquad 45$$

QUESTION 2

The balance bar is balancing exactly. Using the equation, work out the value of *b*.

$$10b \qquad = \qquad 90$$

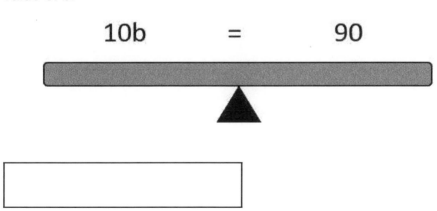

QUESTION 3

The balance bar is balancing exactly. Using the equation, work out the value of *y*.

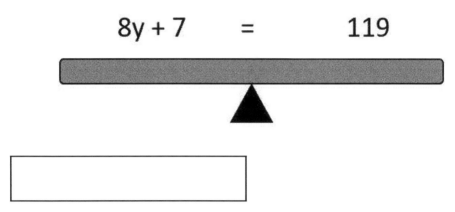

$$8y + 7 \quad = \quad 119$$

QUESTION 4

The balance bar is balancing exactly. Using the equation, work out the value of *y*.

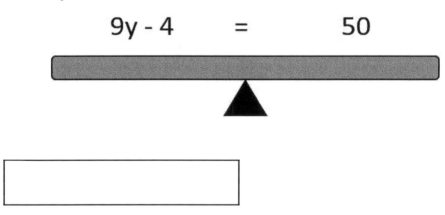

$$9y - 4 \quad = \quad 50$$

QUESTION 5

If $a = 6$ and $b = 7$, work out the answer to the equation. Write your answer in the box on the balance bar.

$$4a + 6b \quad =$$

QUESTION 6

If $a = 9$, $b = 3$ and $c = 2$, work out the answer to the equation. Write your answer in the box on the balance bar.

$$2(a + b) \times c \quad =$$

QUESTION 7

If $a = 4$, $b = 6$ and $c = 12$, work out the answer to the equation. Write your answer in the box on the balance bar.

$$4(c - b) + a \quad =$$

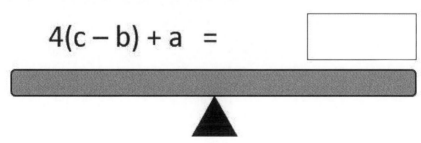

Answers

Q1.

$a = 34$

- $45 - 11 = 34$

- $a = 34$

Q2.

$b = 9$

- $90 \div 10 = 9$

- $b = 9$

Q3.

$y = 14$

- $8y \, (-7) = 119 \, (-7)$

- $8y = 112$

- $112 \div 8 = 14$

- $y = 14$

Q4.

y = 6

- 9y (+4) = 50 (+4)

- 9y = 50 (+4)

- 9y = 54

- 54 ÷ 9 = 6

- y = 6

Q5.

66

- (4 x 6) + (6 x 7)

- 24 + 42 = 66

Q6.

48

- 2(9 + 3) x 2

- 2(12) x 2

- 24 x 2 = 48

Q7.

28

- 4(12 - 6) + 4

- 4(6) + 4

- 24 + 4 = 28

HOW ARE YOU GETTING ON?

SOLVING EQUATIONS

(INTRODUCTION TO EQUATIONS)

SOLVING EQUATIONS

Now that you've learnt the basics of equations, and how to balance them out, you should be quite a WIZARD at solving equations.

Although you've solved lots of basic equations already, now's the time to learn the step-by-step process of how to solve more complicated equations.

Before I move on, let's recap on some of the golden nuggets that you MUST remember.

GOLDEN NUGGETS

1. Whatever you do to one side of the equation, you must do to the other side.

2. Often, you will need to get rid of something on one side, to work out the missing value. To get rid of something, you must do the opposite to what it is saying (if the equation uses a +, you will -. If the equation uses a ÷, you will x.)

3. You will need to keep getting rid of values, until you are left with one letter.

EXAMPLE 1

Solve the equation:

$$5y + 6 = 41$$

Step 1 = We want to get the y on its own, so we need to remove the +6. To remove the +6, we must move it to the other side of the equals sign and do the OPPOSITE.

- $5y = 41 - 6$

- $5y = 35$

Step 2 = We now know that $5y$ is equivalent to 35. We need to work out the value of one y.

- $35 \div 5 = 7$

- $y = 7$

EXAMPLE 2

Solve the equation:

$$4x - 7 = 3x + 2$$

Step 1 = First of all, we need to get $4x$ on its own. To do this, we need to move the -7 to the other side of the equals sign. That means we must add it.

- $4x = 3x + 2 + 7$

- $4x = 3x + 9$

Step 2 = Now, we need to move all of the x values onto one side. We need to move the $3x$ to the other side of the equals sign. That means the $+3x$ will become $-3x$.

- $4x - 3x = 9$

- $1x = 9$

- $x = 9$

Question Time!

QUESTION 1

Solve the equation:

$$3x = (2 + 2x) + 5$$

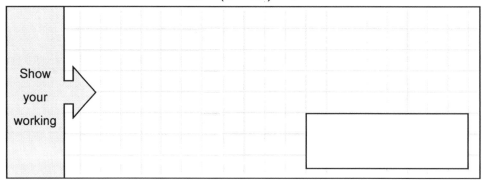

Show
your
working

QUESTION 2

Solve the equation:

$$8y - 1 = 6y - 5$$

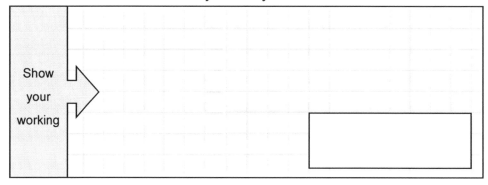

Show
your
working

QUESTION 3

Solve the equation:

$$9(3a - 5) = 9$$

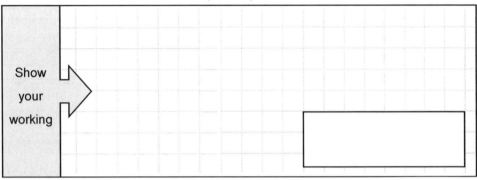

QUESTION 4

Solve the equation:

$$2(4b + 7) - 2b = 3(3b) - 10$$

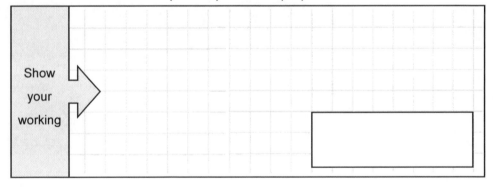

QUESTION 5

Solve the equation:

$$\frac{x + 20}{2} = 17$$

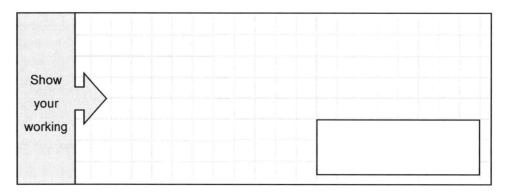

Show your working

QUESTION 6

Solve the equation:

$$\frac{4y - 7}{9} = 5$$

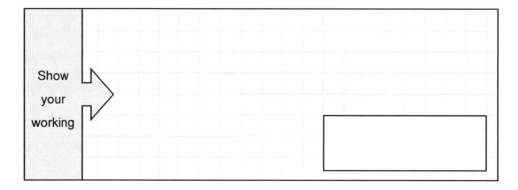

Show your working

Answers

Q1.

$x = 7$

- $3x = 2x + 2 + 5$
- $1x = 2 + 5$
- $x = 7$

Q2.

$y = -2$

- $8y = 6y - 5 + 1$
- $8y = 6y - 4$
- $2y = -4$
- $y = -2$

Q3.

$a = 2$

- $27a - 45 = 9$
- $27a = 9 + 45$
- $27a = 54$
- $a = 2$

Q4.

$b = 8$

- $8b + 14 - 2b = 9b - 10$
- $8b + 24 - 2b = 9b$
- $8b - 2b = 6b$
- $24 = 9b - 6b = 3b$
- $b = 8$

Q5.

$x = 14$

- $17 \times 2 = 34$
- $34 - 20 = 14$
- $x = 14$

Q6.

$y = 13$

- $9 \times 5 = 45$
- $45 + 7 = 52$
- $52 = (4 \times 13)$
- $y = 13$

SIMULTANEOUS EQUATIONS

(INTRODUCTION TO EQUATIONS)

SIMULTANEOUS EQUATIONS

Simultaneous equations are a little bit more tricky to get your head around.

The difference between the equations we have previously worked through, and simultaneous equations, is that simultaneous equations require you to work out two unknown values.

To work out the unknown values, you will need to work out two equations at the same time; finding out what the value of x and y is.

EXAMPLE 1

Solve the simultaneous equations and work out the value of x and y.

$$2x + y = 14$$

$$4x - y = 16$$

How to work it out:

- To try and solve a simultaneous equation, you must try to eliminate one of the unknown values.

- Let's begin by eliminating y (because $+y$ and $-y$ means there is 0 y.)

  $6x = 30$

  $x = 5 \ (30 \div 6)$

- Now, using the value of x, you will be able to work out the value of y.

  $2x \ (2 \times 5) + y = 14$

  $y = 4$

- You can double check your answers by putting the answer back in to the equation, and seeing if they work for both equations.

Question Time!

QUESTION 1

Solve the simultaneous equations, and work out the value of x and y.

$$4x + 2y = 22$$

$$6x - 2y = 28$$

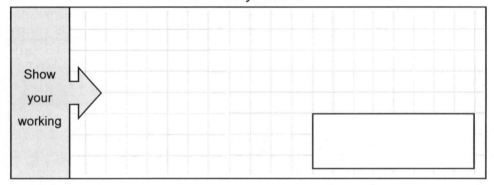

Show your working

QUESTION 2

Solve the simultaneous equations and work out the value of a and b.

$$2a + 5b = 33$$

$$a + 3b = 19$$

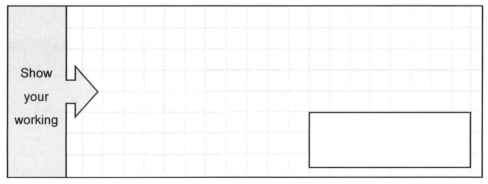

Show your working

QUESTION 3

Solve the simultaneous equations and work out the value of a and b.

$$4a - 6b = 0$$

$$6a + 2b = 22$$

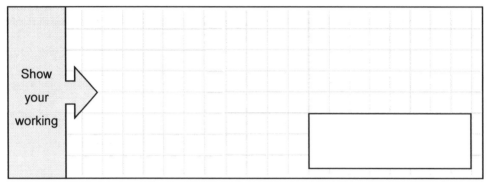

QUESTION 4

Solve the simultaneous equations and work out the value of x and y.

$$x + 2y = 22$$

$$-x + 5y = 27$$

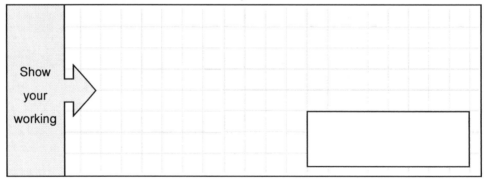

Answers

Q1.

$x = 5$ $y = 1$

- Eliminate y
- $10x = 50$

$x = 5$

- $(4 \times 5) + 2y = 22$
- $22 + (2 \times 1) = 22$

$y = 1$

Q2.

$a = 4$ $b = 5$

- $2a + 5b = 33$
- $a + 3b = 19$ $(2a + 6b = 38)$
- $2a + 5b = 33$
- $2a + 6b = 38$

$b = 5$

- $(5 \times 5) + 2a = 33$
- $25 + 2a = 33$
- $33 - 25 = 8$ $(8 \div 2 = 4)$

$a = 4$

Q3.

$a = 3$ $\quad b = 2$

- $4a - 6b = 0$ (x3)
- $6a - 2b = 22$ (x2)
- $12a + 18b = 0$
- $12a + 4b = 44$
- $22b = 44$

$b = 2$

- $4a - (6 \times 2) = 0$
- $4a - 12 = 0$
- $(4 \times 3) - 12 = 0$

$a = 3$

Q4.

$x = 8$ $\quad y = 7$

- $x + 2y = 22$
- $-x + 5y = 27$
- $7y = 49$

$y = 7$

- $(2 \times 7) + x = 22$
- $14 + x = 22$

$x = 8$

HOW ARE YOU GETTING ON?

UNDERSTANDING INEQUALITIES

INEQUALITIES

(INTRODUCTION TO INEQUALITIES)

UNDERSTANDING INEQUALITIES

As the name suggests, 'inequalities' refers to symbols that do not show EQUAL values.

LEARN YOUR INEQUALITIES!

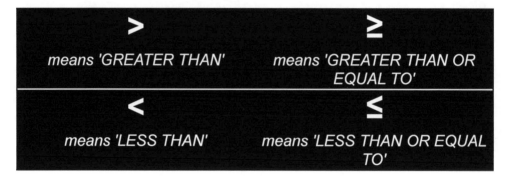

>	≥
means 'GREATER THAN'	*means 'GREATER THAN OR EQUAL TO'*
<	≤
means 'LESS THAN'	*means 'LESS THAN OR EQUAL TO'*

A cool way to remember the different symbols...

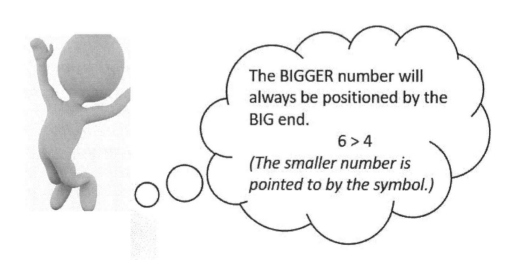

The BIGGER number will always be positioned by the BIG end.

6 > 4

(The smaller number is pointed to by the symbol.)

EXAMPLES

1. $x < 8$

- This means that 'x' is LESS THAN 8.
- The possibilities of the value of x are: 7, 6, 5, 4, 3, 2, 1

2. $-5 < x$

- This means that '-5' is LESS THAN the value of x.
- The possibilities of the value of x are: -4, -3, -2, -1 and so forth

> **Sometimes, there may be more than one inequality.**

3. $-4 < x \leq 3$

- This means that 'x' is MORE THAN -4. It also means that 'x' is LESS THAN OR EQUAL TO 3.
- The possibilities of the value of x are: -3, -2, -1, 0, 1, 2, 3

4. $4 < x < 8$

- This means that 'x' is MORE THAN 4. It also means that 'x' is LESS THAN 8.
- The possibilities of the value of x are: 5, 6, 7

Question Time!

QUESTION 1

Match the symbol with its correct definition.

<   ≤   ≥   >

| MORE THAN OR EQUAL TO | LESS THAN | MORE THAN | LESS THAN OR EQUAL TO |

QUESTION 2

Write down all of the possible values of y in the inequality.

$$-5 < y < 4$$

_____

_____

_____

QUESTION 3

Write down all of the possible values of x in the inequality.

$$5 \le x \le 14$$

_____

_____

_____

QUESTION 4

Write down the first six values of n in the inequality.

$$-6 < n$$

_____

_____

_____

QUESTION 5

Write down all of the possible values of x in the inequality.

$$-1 < x \le 4$$

_____

_____

_____

Answers

Q1.

< = less than

> = greater than

≤ = less than or equal to

≥ = more than or equal to

Q2.

-4, -3, -2, -1, 0, 1, 2, 3

- This means that *y* is more than -5, but less than 4.
- So the possible values of *y* are: -4, -3, -2, -1, 0, 1, 2, 3

Q3.

5, 6, 7, 8, 9, 10, 11, 12, 13, 14

- This means that *x* is more than or equal to 5, but less than or equal to 14.
- So the possible values of *x* are: 5, 6, 7, 8, 9, 10, 11, 12, 13, 14

Q4.

-5, -4, -3, -2, -1, 0

This means that *n* is more than -6.

So, the first 6 values of *n* are: -5, -4, -3, -2, -1, 0

Q5.

0, 1, 2, 3, 4

This means that x is more than -1, but less than or equal to 4.

So the possible values of x are: 0, 1, 2, 3, 4

INEQUALITIES AND NUMBER LINES

(INTRODUCTION TO INEQUALITIES)

INEQUALITIES AND NUMBER LINES

When working with inequalities, you can also use number lines to represent the same information.

Drawing a number line is really simple! However, there are a few things that you need to remember.

- If you use > or <, you will need to use an **open circle**. An open circle is used because the number is NOT included. ○

- If you use ≤ or ≥, you will need to use a **coloured-in circle**. A coloured-in circle is used because the number IS included. ●

EXAMPLES

1. $-3 < x \le 2$

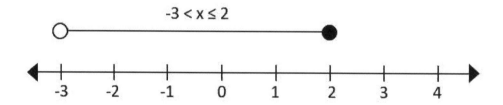

2. $-3 \le x \le 3$

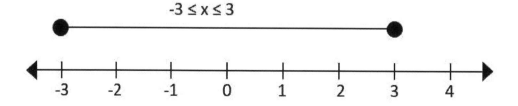

Question Time!

QUESTION 1

Draw the following inequality on the number line.

$$-4 < x < 5$$

QUESTION 2

Draw the following inequality on the number line.

$$-3 \leq y \leq 1$$

QUESTION 3

Draw the following inequality on the number line.

$$-1 < n < 5$$

QUESTION 4

Based on the number line, write down the inequality for x.

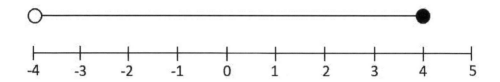

Inequality = _____

QUESTION 5

Based on the number line, write down the inequality for x.

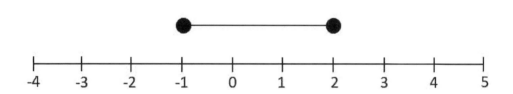

Inequality = _____

QUESTION 6

Based on the number line, write down the inequality for x.

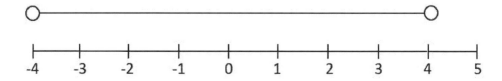

Inequality = _____

Answers

Q1.

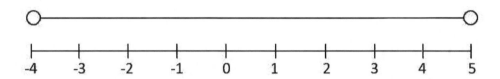

Q2.

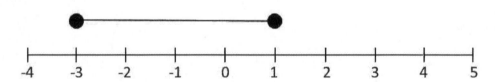

Q3.

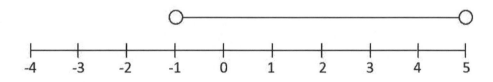

Q4.

-4 < *x* ≤ 4

Q5.

-1 ≤ *x* ≤ 2

Q6.

-4 < *x* < 4

SOLVING INEQUALITIES

(INTRODUCTION TO INEQUALITIES)

SOLVING INEQUALITIES

Sometimes, you may be required to rearrange the inequality in order to solve it.

EXAMPLE 1

Solve the inequality:

$$4x + 1 < 37$$

How to work it out:

- In order to solve this inequality, you need to begin by getting the x value on its own.

- We can move the '+1' to the other side, which then becomes '-1'.

  $4x < 36$

- To find x, you now need to divide each side by 4:

  $x < 9$

EXAMPLE 2

Solve the inequality:

$$9y - 1 < 53$$

How to work it out:

- In order to solve this inequality, you need to begin by getting the y value on its own.

- We can move the '-1' to the other side, which then becomes '+1'.

  $9y < 54$

- To find y, you now need to divide each side by 9:

  $y < 6$

Question Time!

QUESTION 1

Work out the solution of the inequality.

$$8y + 6 > 54$$

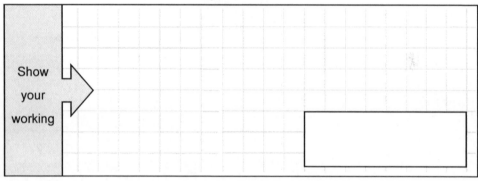

Show your working

QUESTION 2

Work out the solution of the inequality.

$$12x - 14 > 82$$

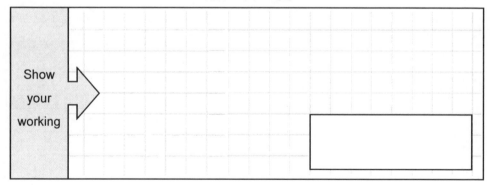

Show your working

QUESTION 3

Work out the solution of the inequality.

$$20y + 60 < 180$$

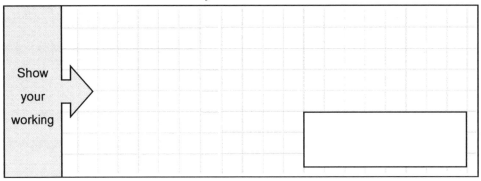

QUESTION 4

Work out the solution of the inequality.

$$16n - 4 > 140$$

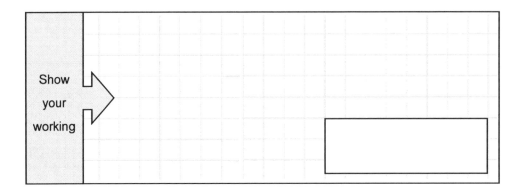

Answers

Q1.

y > 6

- $8y > 54 - 6$
- $8y > 48$
- $y > 6$

Q2.

x > 8

- $12x > 82 + 14$
- $12x > 96$
- $x > 8$

Q3.

y < 6

- $20y < 180 - 60$
- $20y < 120$
- $y < 6$

Q4.

$n > 9$

- $16n > 140 + 4$
- $16n > 144$
- $n > 9$

NUMBER PATTERNS

(PATTERNS AND SEQUENCES)

NUMBER PATTERNS

A number pattern is a sequence of numbers that follow a rule.

There are lots of different number patterns that you should familiarise yourselves with, and these include the following:

- Even and odd numbers
- Prime numbers
- Square numbers
- Cube numbers
- Triangle numbers
- Multiples

EVEN AND ODD NUMBERS

This is very basic, and you should already know the difference between even and odd numbers.

- An **even number** is any number that can be divided by 2. If a number ends in <u>2, 4, 6, 8 or 0</u>, then it is an even number.
- An **odd number** is a number that cannot be divided by 2. If a number ends in <u>1, 3, 5, 7 or 9</u>, then it is an odd number.

No matter how big the number is, you will quickly be able to work out whether it is odd or even - based on the last digit!

Use the bullet points above to work out whether the last digit means the number is odd or even.

PRIME NUMBERS

A prime number is a number (greater than 1) that can only be divided by 1 and itself. For example:

- 7 is a prime number, because it can only be divided by 1 and 7.
- 11 is a prime number, because it can only be divided by 1 and 11.

The circled numbers are the prime numbers up to 100.

1	**2**	**3**	4	**5**	6	**7**	8	9	10
11	12	**13**	14	15	16	**17**	18	**19**	20
21	22	**23**	24	25	26	27	28	**29**	30
31	32	33	34	35	36	**37**	38	39	40
41	42	**43**	44	45	46	**47**	48	49	50
51	52	**53**	54	55	56	57	58	**59**	60
61	62	63	64	65	66	**67**	68	69	70
71	72	**73**	74	75	76	77	78	**79**	80
81	82	**83**	84	85	86	87	88	**89**	90
91	92	93	94	95	96	**97**	98	99	100

SQUARE NUMBERS

Square numbers are numbers multiplied by itself. They are usually represented by the symbol ^{2}.

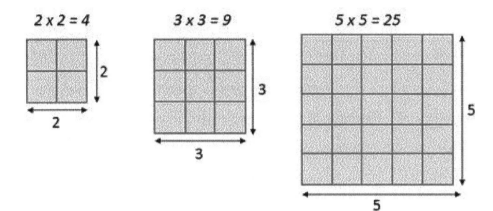

• $1^2 = 1 \times 1 = 1$	•	$5^2 = 5 \times 5 = 25$
• $2^2 = 2 \times 2 = 4$	•	$6^2 = 6 \times 6 = 36$
• $3^2 = 3 \times 3 = 9$	•	$7^2 = 7 \times 7 = 49$
• $4^2 = 4 \times 4 = 16$	•	$8^2 = 8 \times 8 = 64$

CUBE NUMBERS

A cubed number is a number that is multiplied by itself THREE times. This is usually represented by the symbol ^{3}.

$1 \times 1 \times 1 = 1$ $2 \times 2 \times 2 = 8$ $3 \times 3 \times 3 = 27$

 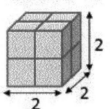 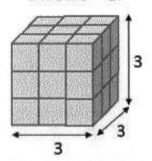

•	$1^3 = 1 \times 1 \times 1 = 1$	•	$5^3 = 5 \times 5 \times 5 = 125$
•	$2^3 = 2 \times 2 \times 2 = 8$	•	$6^3 = 6 \times 6 \times 6 = 216$
•	$3^3 = 3 \times 3 \times 3 = 27$	•	$7^3 = 7 \times 7 \times 7 = 343$
•	$4^3 = 4 \times 4 \times 4 = 64$	•	$8^3 = 8 \times 8 \times 8 = 512$

TRIANGLE NUMBERS

Triangle numbers are exactly that - they form a triangle shape! On the next page are the first few trianglular numbers.

-
- $(1 + 2) = 3$
- $(1 + 2 + 3) = 6$
- $(1 + 2 + 3 + 4) = 10$

MULTIPLES

Multiples are just another word for 'TIMES TABLES'. You need to learn as many of these as you can!

X	1	2	3	4	5	6	7	8	9	10	11	12
1	1	2	3	4	5	6	7	8	9	10	11	12
2	2	4	6	8	10	12	14	16	18	20	22	24
3	3	6	9	12	15	18	21	24	27	30	33	36
4	4	8	12	16	20	24	28	32	36	40	44	48
5	5	10	15	20	25	30	35	40	45	50	55	60
6	6	12	18	24	30	36	42	48	54	60	66	72
7	7	14	21	28	35	42	49	56	63	70	77	84
8	8	16	24	32	40	48	56	64	72	80	88	96
9	9	18	27	36	45	54	63	72	81	90	99	108
10	10	20	30	40	50	60	70	80	90	100	110	120
11	11	22	33	44	55	66	77	88	99	110	121	132
12	12	24	36	48	60	72	84	96	108	120	132	144

As you can see, there are lots of number patterns to look out for.

You should be familiar with all of these, but if not, we recommend that you learn each of these before moving on to more complex sequences such as linear and quadratic sequences.

Have a go at the activity questions on the following pages to make sure you know everything in this chapter!

Question Time!

QUESTION 1

Circle all of the prime numbers.

17   45   49   12   64   91   50   4   5   18   30   15

QUESTION 2

Circle the three squared numbers.

17   45   49   12   64   91   50   4   5   18   30   15

QUESTION 3

Write the first 10 multiples for the following numbers:

a)   9

b)   12

c)   13

QUESTION 4

Which of the numbers below is a square number, a cubed number and a triangle number? <u>Circle one</u>.

36	1	10	42

QUESTION 5

For the following numbers, circle whether they are **odd** or **even**.

a)   3,495   **ODD   /   EVEN**

b)   9,329,432   **ODD   /   EVEN**

c)   12,043,931   **ODD   /   EVEN**

QUESTION 6

Work out the square root of the numbers .

49	4	81	36
_____	_____	_____	_____
121	9	225	144
_____	_____	_____	_____

QUESTION 7

Draw the next 3 triangle numbers using dots. Based on your diagrams, fill in the other half of the table. <u>The first four drawings have been drawn for you.</u>

   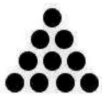

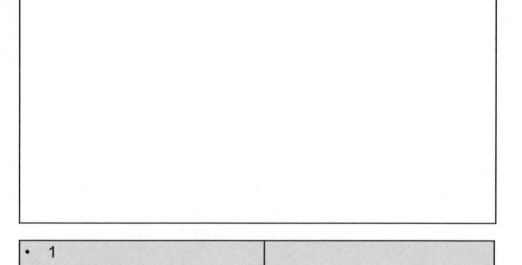

• 1	
• (1 + 2) = 3	
• (1 + 2 + 3) = 6	
• (1 + 2 + 3 + 4) = 10	

Answers

Q1.

17 and 5

- Prime numbers are numbers that can only be divided by 1 and itself.

Q2.

49, 64, 4

- (7 x 7) = 49

- (8 x 8) = 64

- (2 x 2) = 4

Q3.

a) 9, 18, 27, 36, 45, 54, 63, 72, 81, 90

b) 12, 24, 36, 48, 60, 72, 84, 96, 108, 120

c) 13, 26, 39, 52, 65, 78, 91, 104, 117, 130

Q4.

1

- 1 is square number (1 x 1)

- 1 is cube number (1 x 1 x 1)

- 1 is the first number of the triangular numbers.

Q5.

a) odd

b) even

c) odd

Q6.

49	4	81	36
7	2	9	6
121	9	225	144
11	3	15	12

Q7.

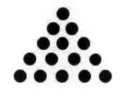 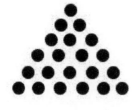 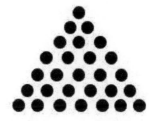

• 1	• (1 + 2 + 3 + 4 + 5) = 15
• (1 + 2) = 3	• (1 + 2 + 3 + 4 + 5 + 6) = 21
• (1 + 2 + 3) = 6	• (1 + 2 + 3 + 4 + 5 + 6 + 7) = 28
• (1 + 2 + 3 + 4) = 10	

HOW ARE YOU GETTING ON?

LINEAR SEQUENCES

(PATTERNS AND SEQUENCES)

LINEAR SEQUENCES

A linear sequence is a number pattern which increases or decreases by the SAME AMOUNT each time.

The number which the sequence increases or decreases by, is called the <u>common difference</u>.

How to work out the rule of a sequence:

- The secret to working out the rule of a sequence is to work out what you have to do to get from one number to the next.

- Once you think you have found the rule, double check that it works for the rest of the sequence.

- Generally, there are two types of sequences to look out for:

  1. **ARITHMETIC SEQUENCES** - adding and subtracting the <u>same number</u>.

  2. **GEOMETRIC SEQUENCES** - multiplying and dividing the <u>same number</u>.

RULE 1 - ADDING THE SAME NUMBER

Number sequences may be progressing by <u>adding</u> the <u>same number</u>.

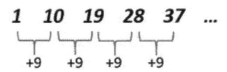

So, the rule for this sequence is to <u>add 9</u>.

RULE 2 - SUBTRACTING THE SAME NUMBER

Number sequences may be progressing by <u>subtracting</u> the <u>same</u> <u>number</u>.

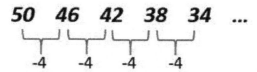

So, the rule for this sequence is to <u>subtract 4</u>.

RULE 3 - MULTIPLYING OR DIVIDING BY THE SAME NUMBER

Number sequences may be progressing by <u>multiplying</u> or <u>dividing</u> by the <u>same number</u>.

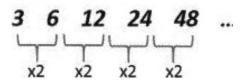

So, the rule for this sequence is to <u>multiply by 2</u>.

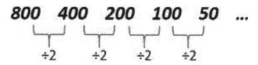

So, the rule for this sequence is <u>divide by 2</u>.

FINDING THE nth TERM

Sometimes, you may be asked questions on sequences that asks you to find the 100th value.

Of course, you are not going to sit there and work out the values for every number from 1 to 100. You need a quick way to work out the value.

There is a simple method to work out the nth term of a sequence, so long as you know the <u>common difference</u> (see page 132 for more information).

EXAMPLE

Find an expression for the nth term of the following sequence:

4   7   10   13   16

<u>How to work it out</u>:

1. First of all, you need to find the common difference. The sequence is progressing by <u>adding 3</u>. So, in the formula you would write 3*n*. '*n*' is the term you are trying to work out.

n	1	2	3	4	5
term	4	7	10	13	16

2. Next, you need to list the values of 3*n*.

3	6	9	12

(3 + 1) = 4   (6 + 1) = 7   (9 + 1) = 10   (12 + 1) = 13

3. Work out what you have to do to get from 3*n* to each term. As you can see, you need to <u>add 1</u>.

So the formula is 3*n* + 1.

Some questions may ask you whether a value would appear in the sequence.

You can work out whether the value would appear in the sequence by factoring in the value into the sequence and working out the value of n.

If n is a whole number, the value **WOULD** appear in the sequence. If n is a decimal or fraction of a number, the value would **NOT** appear in the sequence.

EXAMPLE

Using the rule $4n + 2$, work out whether the term 22 appears in the sequence.

How to work it out:

1. Let's use the rule and place 22 after the equals sign:

   $4n + 2 = 22$

2. That means $4n = 20$. So you need to work out the value of one n.

   $20 \div 4 = 5$

   $n = 5$

3. The value of n is a whole number, which means that 22 **WOULD** appear in this sequence. 22 is the 5th value of the sequence.

REMEMBER TO USE YOUR COMMON SENSE!

Sometimes, you can work out whether a number is going to appear in a sequence based on all of the other numbers in the sequence.

For example, if all of the values in the sequence are even, that means an odd number is not going to appear in the sequence.

Another example, if all the values end in 2 or 7, that means a number ending in 1 is not going to appear in the sequence.

Question Time!

QUESTION 1

Write the next 5 terms in the following linear sequence.

1st term	2nd term	3rd term	4th term	5th term
5	11	17	23	29

6th term	7th term	8th term	9th term	10th term

QUESTION 2

Which two numbers come next in the sequence?

2   4   8   16   32   64

A	B	C	D
126 215	128 256	128 265	182 265

QUESTION 3

Which two numbers come next in the sequence?

185   176   167   158   149

A	B	C	D
141 157	137 222	140 131	135 128

QUESTION 4

Below are four match sticks.

Pattern 1

The pattern continues as follows:

Pattern 1   **Pattern 2**   **Pattern 3**

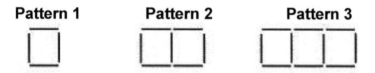

a) How many match sticks would be in pattern 9?

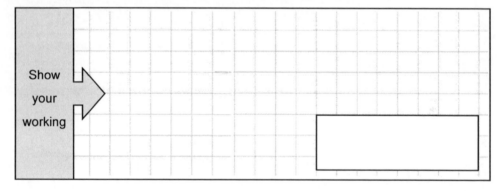

Show your working

b) If *n* represents the number of match sticks, and *p* represents the pattern number, write the rule to work out how the sequence is progressing.

_____

_____

_____

c) Using your answer to part b, work out how many match sticks would be needed for the 85th pattern.

_____

_____

_____

QUESTION 5

Take a look at the following number pattern.

1   2   3   4

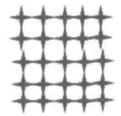

Using the sequence above, fill in the rest of the table.

Pattern number	1st	2nd	3rd	4th	5th	6th	7th
Number of diamonds	1	9	17				

QUESTION 6

The rule you are given is $7n + 9$.

If n represents the nth term in the sequence, what would the 35th term in the seqeunce be?

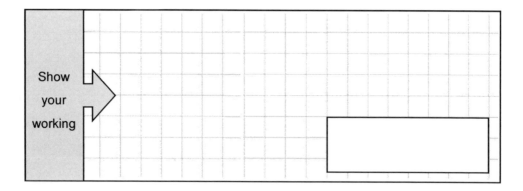

Show your working

QUESTION 7

Write the next 5 terms in the following linear sequence.

1st term	2nd term	3rd term	4th term	5th term
208	197	186	175	164

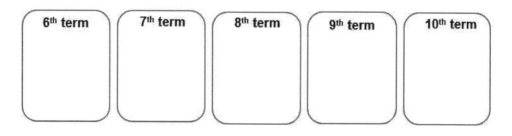

| 6th term | 7th term | 8th term | 9th term | 10th term |

Answers

Q1.

6th term	7th term	8th term	9th term	10th term
35	41	47	53	59

Q2.

B = 128   256

- The sequence is multiplying by 2 each time.

Q3.

C = 140   131

- The sequence is subtracting 9 each time.

Q4.

a) 28

- The number of match sticks is increasing by 3 each.
- To work out the ninth pattern:

  9 x 3 = 27 + 1 = 28

b) number of match sticks (n) = number pattern (p) x 3 + 1

c) 256

- Number of match sticks (85) x 3 + 1
- 85 x 3 = 255
- 255 + 1 = 256

Q5.

Pattern number	1st	2nd	3rd	4th	5th	6th	7th
Number of diamonds	1	9	17	25	33	41	49

Q6.

254

- 7 x 35 = 245
- 245 + 9 = 254

Q7.

6th term	7th term	8th term	9th term	10th term
153	142	131	120	109

HOW ARE YOU GETTING ON?

QUADRATIC SEQUENCES

(PATTERNS AND SEQUENCES)

QUADRATIC SEQUENCES

A quadratic sequence is when the difference between each value is not constant. It becomes a quadratic sequence if the second difference is the same.

The best way to get your head around quadratic sequences is via example.

Take a look at the example below.

EXAMPLE

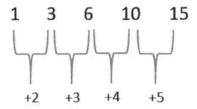

- As you can see, the <u>first difference</u> between each term changes each time.

- However, when looking at the difference, you should realise that these differences are increasing by 1 each time. This is the <u>second difference</u>.

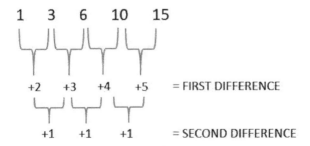

FINDING THE nth TERM

Finding the nth term of a quadratic sequence is a little bit more tricky than linear sequences.

EXAMPLE

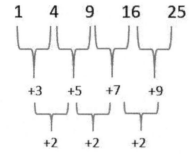

- As you can see, the numbers in the sequence are squared numbers (see page 122).

- The nth term of this sequence is n^2.

NOTE:

If a quadratic sequence has the <u>second difference</u> of 2, that means the sequence will have something to do with n^2.

Question Time!

QUESTION 1

Below is a quadratic sequence.

1st term	2nd term	3rd term	4th term	5th term
3	6	11	18	27

a) Write the next 5 terms in this quadratic sequence.

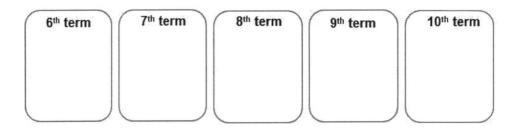

| 6th term | 7th term | 8th term | 9th term | 10th term |

b) Work out the rule to find the nth term in this quadratic sequence.

_____

_____

_____

c) What is the 20th term in this sequence?

_____

_____

QUESTION 2

Below is a quadratic sequence.

1st term	2nd term	3rd term	4th term	5th term
0	2	6	12	20

a) Write the next 5 terms in this quadratic sequence.

6th term	7th term	8th term	9th term	10th term

b) Work out the rule to find the nth term in this quadratic sequence.

_____

_____

_____

c) What is the 30th term in this sequence?

_____

_____

QUESTION 3

Below is a quadratic sequence.

1st term	2nd term	3rd term	4th term	5th term
2 + 3	6 + 3	10 + 3	14 + 3	18 + 3

a) What is the next term in this quadratic sequence?

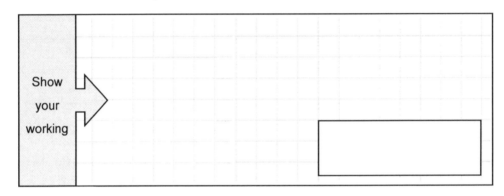

Show your working

b) Work out the rule for this quadratic sequence.

_____

_____

_____

c) What is the 16th term in this quadratic sequence?

_____

_____

_____

Answers

Q1.

a)

6th term	7th term	8th term	9th term	10th term
38	51	66	83	102

b)

$n^2 + 2$

- The second difference in this pattern is adding 2. That means this sequence has something to do with n^2.

- If we add 2 to n^2, we get each term in the sequence.

c)

402

- We have just worked out that the rule for this sequence is $n^2 + 2$.

- If we want to find the 20th term in the sequence, we would factor this into the rule:

20 x 20 = 400

400 + 2 = 402

Q2.

a)

6th term	7th term	8th term	9th term	10th term
30	42	56	72	90

b)

$n^2 - n$

- The <u>second difference</u> in this quadratic sequence is adding 2, so that means the rule will have something to do with n^2.

- For each term, work out what you have to do to the n^2, in order to reach the numbers. For this sequence, you need to subtract the nth term.

c)

870

- We have just worked out that the rule for this sequence is $n^2 - n$.

- If we wanted to find the 30th term in the sequence, we would factor this into the rule:

30 x 30 = 900

900 - 30 = 870

Q3.

a)

22 + 3 OR 25

- The sequence is progressing by adding 4 to the previous term.

b)

4n + 1

- The second difference in this quadratic sequence is adding 4.

- The difference tells us that we need to multiply the nth term by 4, and then add 1.

c)

65

- We have just worked out that the rule for this sequence is 4n + 1.

- If we wanted to find the 16th term in the sequence, we would factor this into the rule:

  4 x 16 = 64

  64 + 1 = 65

HOW ARE YOU GETTING ON ?

UNDERSTANDING COORDINATES

(COORDINATES AND GRAPHS)

UNDERSTANDING COORDINATES

Coordinates are used to show positions on a graph.

You will always have an *X* coordinate and a *Y* coordinate. *X* coordinates are read horizontally, and *y* coordinates are read vertically.

Coordinates are ALWAYS written in alphabetic order (*x, y*)

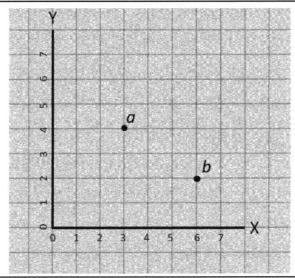

When reading coordinates, it is important that you remember the following:

YOU MUST READ THE COORDINATES ON THE *X* AXIS BEFORE THE *Y* AXIS.

EXAMPLE

In the above graph:

- Point A has the coordinates (3, 4)

- Point B has the coordinates (6, 2)

THE FOUR QUADRANTS

Usually, you will be presented with a graph that has four quadrants.

- In the top right quadrant, coordinates are positive (2, 3)

- In the top left quadrant, the x coordinate will be negative, and the y coordinate will be positive (-1, 2)

- In the bottom right quadrant, the x coordinate will be positive, and the y coordinate will be negative (4, -2)

- In the bottom left quadrant, both coordinates are negative (-5, -4)

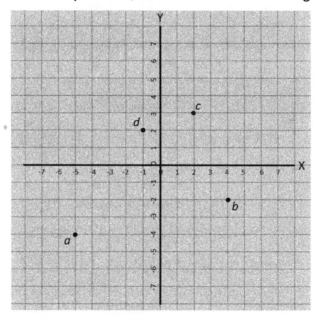

ACTIVITY TIME!

Put your own points on the grid and work out their coordinates!

Question Time!

QUESTION 1

Plot these points on the grid.

- Point A = (3, 2)

- Point B = (2, 3)

- Point C = (3, 4)

- Point D = (4, 3)

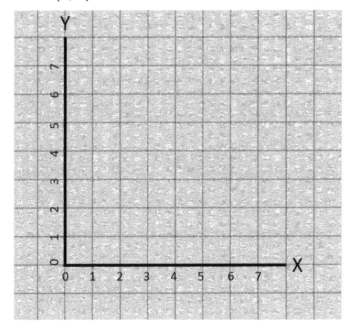

QUESTION 2

For the following statements, circle whether they are true or false.

1. In the bottom right quadrant, the x coordinate will be negative, and the y coordinate will be negative.   **TRUE   /   FALSE**

2. In the top right quadrant, both coordinates are negative.

    TRUE   /   FALSE

3. In the bottom left quadrant, the x coordinate will be positive, and the y coordinate will be negative.   **TRUE   /   FALSE**

4. In the top left quadrant, the x coordinate will be negative, and the y coordinate will be positive .   **TRUE   /   FALSE**

QUESTION 3

Find the words in the wordsearch.

ALONG	AXIS	COORDINATES
GRAPH	NEGATIVE	PLOTTING
POSITIVE	QUADRANTS	REGIONS

```
S F H W I S S K V A U N R P K
B T X S Q E I O H S S E U L Z
G N O L A T X P D P G R L O Q
O O Q B Q A A M O I A Q Y T Q
T N O C R N A L O S D R J T H
S B S I R I E N N P I S G I U
F M U K E D S J B G T T Y N I
I V C P U R A Y Y N L C I G W
Z E S Z F O Y H A W S E W V T
T N S Q X O V R S C H H O B E
D Y N T K C D N E G A T I V E
H I F Y I A F Q T V J N I P P
L S G H U N H I I C Z F Q H D
W W J Q V H F V G Q M F T K Q
T M T J L A K X O N L I B Z N
```

QUESTION 4

Give the coordinates of shape A.

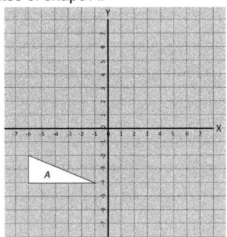

QUESTION 5

Plot these coordinates on the graph.

(-1, -3)   (2, -3)   (3, 1)   (0, 1)

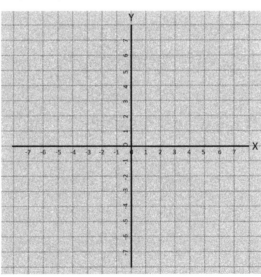

Answers

Q1.

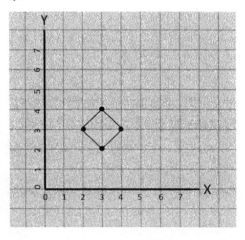

Q2.

1. In the bottom right quadrant, the *x* coordinate will be negative, and the *y* coordinate will be negative.   **FALSE**

2. In the top right quadrant, both coordinates are negative.   **FALSE**

3. In the bottom left quadrant, the *x* coordinate will be positive, and the *y* coordinate will be negative.   **FALSE**

4. In the top left quadrant, the *x* coordinate will be negative, and the *y* coordinate will be positive .   **TRUE**

Q3.

```
S F H W I S S K V A U N R P K
B T X S Q E I O H S S E U L Z
G N O L A T X P D P G R L Q Q
O O Q B Q A A M Q I A Q Y T Q
T N O C R N A L Q S D R J T H
S B S I R I E N N P I S G I U
F M U K E D S J B G T T Y N I
I V C P U R A Y Y N L C I G W
Z E S Z F Q Y H A W S E W V T
T N S Q X Q V R S C H H O B E
D Y N T K C D N E G A T I V E
H I F Y I A F Q T V J N I P P
L S G H U N H I I C Z F Q H D
W W J Q V H F V G Q M F T K Q
T M T J L A K X O N L I B Z N
```

Q4.

(-6, -2)   (-6, -4)   (-1, -4)

Q5.

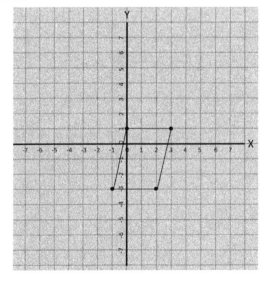

HOW ARE YOU GETTING ON?

PLOTTING AND INTERPRETING GRAPHS

(COORDINATES AND GRAPHS)

STRAIGHT LINES
(Horizontal and Vertical Lines)

Straight lines in the form of:
X = coordinate (c) Y = coordinate (c)

Straight lines in the form of $x = c$ or $y = c$ will create a horizontal or vertical line.

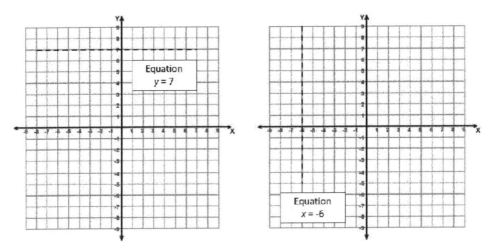

- In the first graph, all the points on the dotted line have the y coordinate of 7. So, the equation of the line is $y = 7$.

- In the second graph, all the points on the dotted line have the x coordinate of -6. So, the equation of the line is $x = -6$.

REMEMBER

All vertical lines will have the equation $x = ...$

All horizontal lines will have the equation $y = ...$

The easiest way to work out whether it is x or y, is to look at where the line crosses through the graph.

Does it cross the x axis or the y axis?

STRAIGHT LINES
(Diagonal Lines)

Diagonal lines in the form of:

$$Y = X \qquad Y = -X$$

Diagonal lines in the form of $y = x$ or $y = -x$ will create a main diagonal.

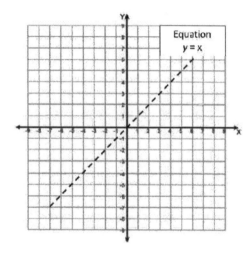

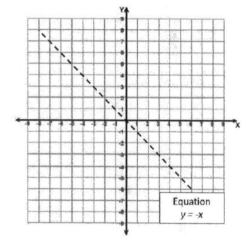

- In the first graph, all the x and y coordinates are the same. So, the equation of the line is $y = x$.

- In the second graph, the x and y coordinates are negatives to each other. If the x coordinate is positive, the y coordinate is negative, and vice versa. So, the equation of the line is $y = -x$.

STRAIGHT LINES
(Lines Through The Origin)

Lines through the origin of a graph:

$$y = ax \qquad y = -ax$$

('a' referring to a number)

The value of 'a' is the gradient which tells you how steep the line is. The form $y = ax$ and $y = -ax$ are equations which show a sloping line.

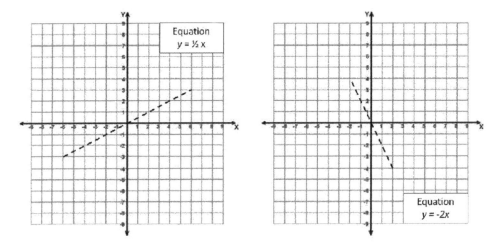

Equation
$y = \frac{1}{2}x$

Equation
$y = -2x$

- In the first graph, the coordinates for x of the dotted line is double the coordinate of y. So, the equation of the line is $y = \frac{1}{2}x$.

- In the second graph, the coordinates show that $y = -2x$.

TABLES AND GRAPHS
(Plotting The Values)

The best way to work out the values of *x* and *y* is to draw up a table.

EXAMPLE

Draw the graph to represent $y = 3x + 1$. Your graph should include values -4 to 3.

Step 1 = Work out the first 3 values of the equation. It helps to lay out your values using a table.

x	0	1	2	3
y				

If x = 0	If x = 1	If x = 2	If x = 3
y = (3 x 0) + 1	y = (3 x 1) + 1	y = (3 x 2) + 1	y = (3 x 3) + 1
y = 1	y = 4	y = 7	y = 10

- Now, you have the coordinates of (0, 1), (1, 4), (2, 7) and (3, 10)
- You can use these to draw your graph, remembering to draw the line so that it covers the range of -4 to 3 - like the question says!

Question Time!

QUESTION 1

Which graph shows this function? Tick the box to show your answer.

$$y = x + 8$$

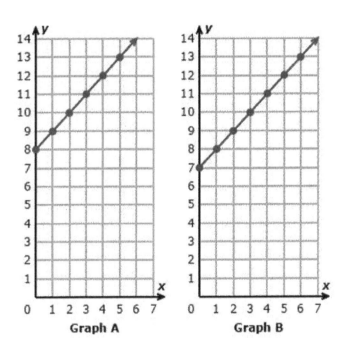

Graph A   Graph B

Graph A ☐

Graph B ☐

QUESTION 2

a) Circle the correct equation that represents line A.

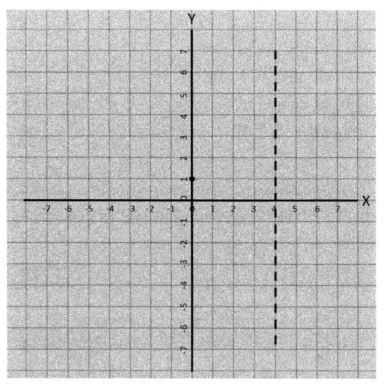

| $y = x + 4$ | $x = 4$ | $x + y = 4$ | $y = 4$ |

b) On the graph above, draw the line for $x + y = 5$

Label this line $x + y = 5$.

c) On the graph above, draw the line for $y = \frac{1}{2}x$

Label this line $y = \frac{1}{2}x$

QUESTION 3

On the graph below, plot the values which represent the line $x + y = 4$ with values of x from -1 to 4.

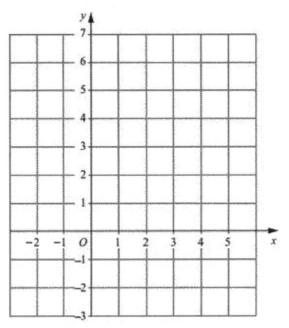

QUESTION 4

What is the equation of the line?

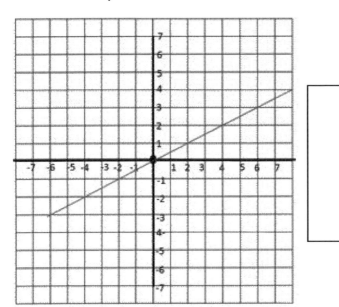

EQUATION

QUESTION 5

Draw the line $y = x + 3$ on the graph below.

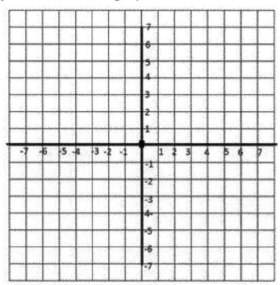

QUESTION 6

Using the equaton $y = 3x - 2$, complete the values in the table below.

x	0	1	2	3	4
y					

Answers

Q1.

Graph A

- $y = x + 8$

- $10 = 2 + 8$

Q2.

a) x = 4

b)

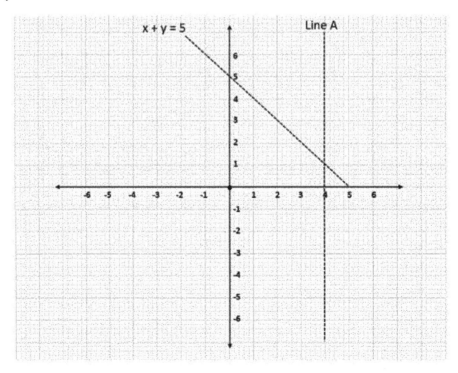

c)

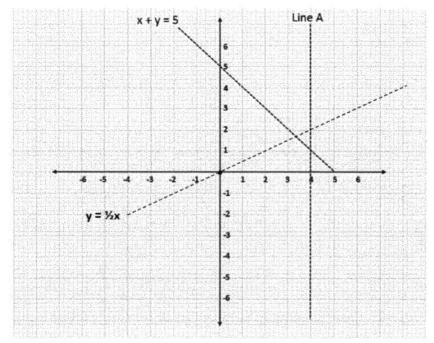

Q3.

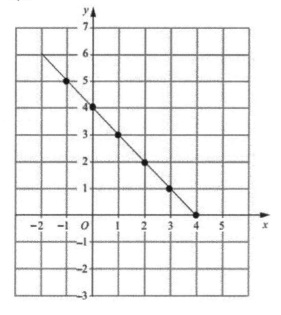

Q4.

y = ½x

Q5.

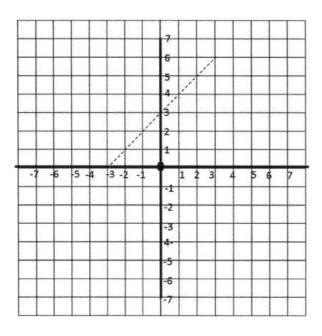

Q6.

x	0	1	2	3	4
y	-2	1	4	7	10

NEED A LITTLE EXTRA HELP WITH KEY STAGE THREE (KS3) MATHS?

How2Become have created these other FANTASTIC guides to help you and your child prepare for their Key Stage Three (KS3) Maths assessments.

FOR MORE INFORMATION ON OUR KEY STAGE 3 (KS3) MATHS GUIDES, PLEASE CHECK OUT THE FOLLOWING:

WWW.HOW2BECOME.COM

WANT TO TAKE A LOOK AT OUR KEY STAGE THREE (KS3) ENGLISH GUIDES?

WWW.HOW2BECOME.COM

Get Access To

FREE

Key Stage 3

Resources

www.MyEducationalTests.co.uk

16488134R00096

Printed in Great Britain
by Amazon